CHAMELEON
DAYS

**The camouflaged and changing emotions
of a woman unleashed**

K.L. LOVELEY

Illustrated by Elvina Dulac

Globeflower
Books

Poetry copyright © 2018 K.L. Loveley

Illustrations copyright © 2018 Elvina Dulac

All rights reserved.
No part of this publication may be reproduced, distributed, or transmitted in any form or by any means, including photocopying, recording, or other electronic or mechanical methods, without the prior written permission of the publisher, except in the case of brief quotations embodied in critical reviews and certain other noncommercial uses permitted by copyright law. For permission requests, write to the publisher, addressed "Attention: Permissions Coordinator," at the address below.

Globeflower Books™

An imprint of The Globeflower Agency
Studio 12, Coventry Canal Warehouse, Leicester Row, Coventry, CV1 4LH.

Front cover illustration Copyright © Elvina Dulac

A CIP catalogue record of this book is available in the British Library

Chameleon Days/ K.L Loveley. -- 1st ed.

ISBN: 978-1-9998294-8-3

Dedication

For my mum Dorothy.

I dedicate this collection of poems to you mum, in your eighty-ninth year of life. As a young mother your life was filled with the joy of your home and family. No time for the simple pleasure of listening to poetry or reading of love. One of the many delights of growing older, is having the time to enjoy the simple pleasures of life. Surrounded by your children, grandchildren and now great-grandchildren, your life has taken on a new meaning. Your interest in my writing career has touched me; allowing my own reflection of life to develop.

The times I have spent with you, reading my work out loud, as you sit in that old familiar chair, smiling. Has given me pleasure indeed. Thank you mum.

"Watch your thoughts, for they become words,
Watch your words, for they become actions,
Watch your actions, for they become habits,
Watch your character, for it becomes your destiny."
Anonymous

Contents

And Now	1
Playing Games	3
Hope	4
Missing You	5
Where Has She Gone?	6
Unexpected	8
Lip Service	9
Feelings	10
Chemistry	11
Release Me	12
To Die For You	13
Sun, Moon, and Stars	14
Confusion	16
Magnetism	17
Infection	18
Which One	19
Another Chapter Closes	20
Mind Reading	22

Frustration	23
Philosophy	24
Children	26
Bereavement	27
Vulnerable	28
Those Bones, Old Bones	29
Decision Time	30
Moving On	31
Olfactory Delights	32
Lazy Dave	33
Autumn Antics	34
Chameleon Days	36

And Now

Life was unreal.

And now…

From the hollowness of time,
the point of it all is clear.
The path of life is planned,
the seeds sown when my life began,
as the two seeds, I grew will follow their own destiny
this is what I hold dear.

And now...

The pain was worth the pleasure and joy,
life's garden affected by the seasons does change.
Transition from first love to awakening of true self,
is but a revelation.

Discovery of self-esteem, of worthiness,
sprung forth provoked by the action of others.
Is like a new flower growing,
where once the ground was choked with weeds.

And now…

Innocence, experience, chemistry.
One glance a bee attracted to the nectar.
Enzymes had no place,
sunlight was not needed,

the flower opened - nature superseded.

The glow - the aura was so strong.
Love again was awoken,
Having been buried by the soil, so long.

And now…

The love remains fixed forever in the seeds,
Dispersed by nature once again,
Be patient - wait for the seasons to change.

The warm air has arrived,
A new sun has arisen,
Old cobwebs are fragile - easy to be swept away,
Like leaves at the end of an autumn day.

Playing Games

Just one look - the game was set,
the pattern would follow
like a set of instructions
imprinted in your brain.

Rules would be contracted,
not to be broken,
others had tried,
of this you had spoken.

This one is different, you said,
This one is special,
No mistakes please,
I don't want to lose you!

The pace - it was racy,
proposal came too fast,
doubts entered your mind,
this model would not last.

Just like all the others.
Not special after all - perhaps a new design,
maybe another catch.
One more relationship over,
game, set, and match.

Hope

Why does he feel so affected by me?
When you are not touched at all.

Why does my voice, the sound, the tone,
give him pleasure enough, just over the phone?

I understand how he feels - for I feel the same.
To hear your voice, or the mention of your name,
flutters my chest - releases endorphins from my brain.
Creates a flush to my cheeks and twinkling in my eyes,
temporary pleasure - released then tucked neatly away,
hibernating inside for another day.

Postcards from abroad - love notes from close to home.
Flowers and gifts - invitations by the score.
Constant hope of a meeting - if only by chance,
the remote possibility of a close up dance.

How can I hurt him when I know how it feels?
Rejection is painful - they say that time heals.
Do I want to be healed, not if these feelings I'd lose?

Am I to dream all of my life, or only if I choose.
Hand me a crystal ball, pass the tarot cards,
should I give myself to the Gods?
Should I read my horoscope?
Perhaps like him - I should not lose all hope.

Missing You

The Irish Sea between us,
the land, the rivers, and roads,
the seconds, the minutes, and hours.
Days that never end.

Nights are being wasted,
precious time should be enjoyed,
life is short enough, before the final void.
This has become apparent, painfully been exposed,
as loved ones are taken from us,
to travel that lonely road.

The land you adore, where your loved one still sleeps,
Is it the place you want to be?
And when you return from this sacred place,
you will again be separated by the Irish Sea.

Where Has She Gone?

Where has she gone, that plain young girl?
Undistinguished - camouflaged by the crowd,
no angel looks - no glossy mane.
Just big brown eyes and bony frame.

Where has she gone?

Young she did look when inappropriate,
others dazzled, sparkled, shone,
blossomed into womanhood,
no not her - childlike she did remain.

Average height and average looks,
fashion clothes, then study books.
Use of pen instead of charm,
deferred gratification does no harm.

But fun she had along the way,
looked radiant on her wedding day.
No compliments - no flattery,
hidden talents not on display.

Bellies round and fading looks,
varicose veins and sick in guts,
babies crying, sleepless nights,
marriages broken, endless fights.

And now the others round and dull,
make way for this chameleon,
still small and slim no longer plain,
now it is her turn for the mating game.

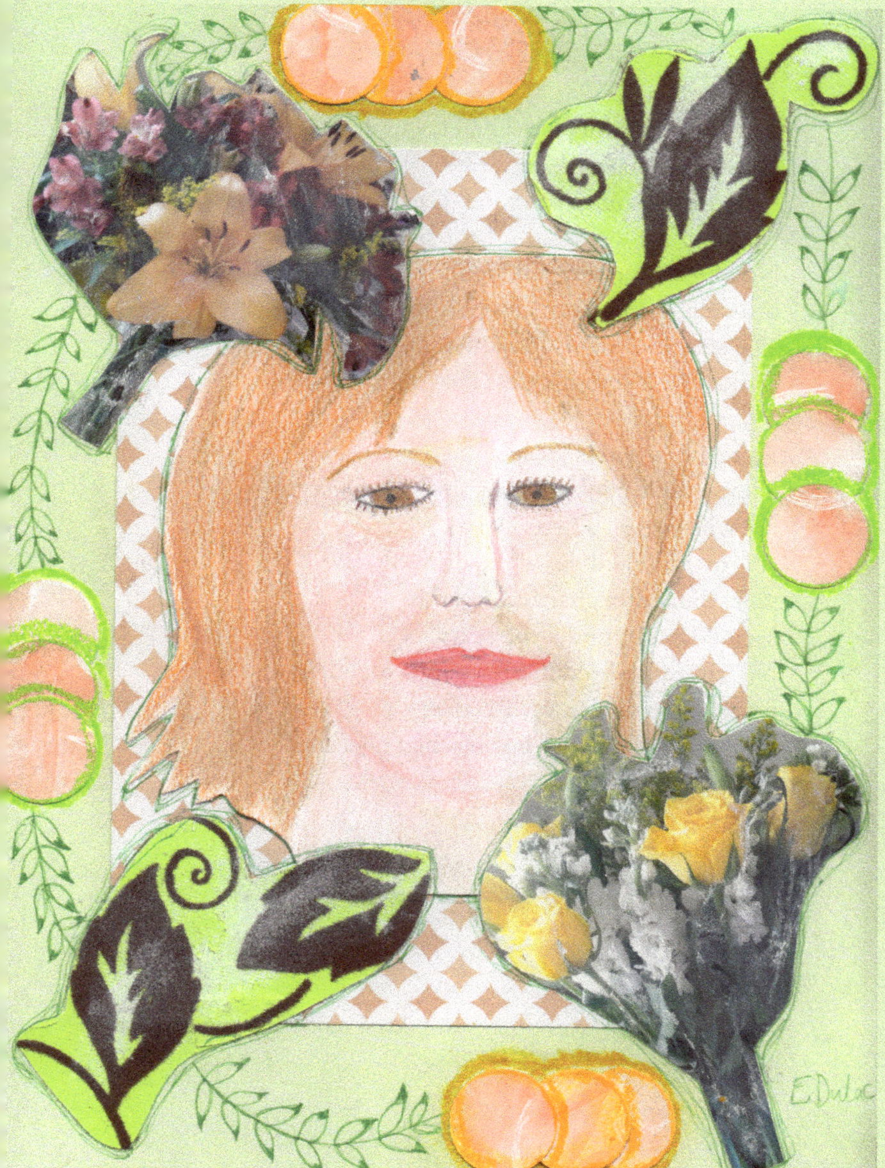

Unexpected

The wounds in my heart had begun to heal,
the scars though fragile were beginning
to fade like ripples from the distant source.

No longer were my waking thoughts
drowning with your name.
The sleepless nights became calm,
settled like a smooth glass lake.

So fragile was this façade
a tiny breeze could destroy this tranquillity,
the whispers of a breeze came.
As you hummed down the diamond line
unleashing thoughts and feelings,
secured neatly under the scars.
No sutures to hold these wounds together,
no saline to wash away the pain.
One word from your lips reached my ears,
and set me off again.

Lip Service

Sweet words sugar coated like almonds
fall from your lips,
saccharine like, is closer to the truth.

For substitute words are only analogues
manufactured to please.
Perfection in this art, you have gained,
word perfect, spell check,
you've practised it all.
Windows to the heart, signals to the brain,
subliminal messages, focused on the psyche
to penetrate for lasting effect.

I listen to your words, wanting to believe,
knowing you have played this game before.
To past unsuspecting lovers,
many have listened to your musical words.
Strings and attachments have been broken,
the pain extinguished
by the sweet words you have spoken.

Feelings

That overpowering feeling took me by surprise,

such was the strength and passion.

Emotions on a high,

to climb into an aeroplane,

strap silk upon my back,

throw my arms up to the heavens.

Step lightly from the edge,

float through the clouds so lightly,

with contentment unbound

then declare my love forever,

as my feet, they touch the ground.

Chemistry

I close my eyes, I think of you,
your name is on my lips.
The sleepless night before me lies,
sweet memories, long lingering sighs.
And when I wake, I feel the same,
my waking thought, remains your name.

Throughout the day a million thoughts
transcend throughout my brain.
My nursing tasks by memory done,
thoughts of you consume my day,
although, one could never tell.

Who would believe a chemistry so strong?
Alas! The equilibrium cannot be reached.
So, what are these chemicals reacting so well?
Not exactly Adonis, or Venus am I.
And yet, a volatile solution creating sparks of fire
creates in me, a passion and desire.

Maybe I'm in love with the memory,
forgetting the sadness and pain.
The constant rejections, over and over again,
is there a more potent element?
One that's meant to be,
out there in the wings of the universe,
waiting just for me.

Release Me

I need to feel anger,
I need to feel pain
to put things in perspective,
to start my life again.

Erase you from my memory, to initiate the start,
remove you forever, from my over generous heart.
Make way for my new love, who is waiting in the wings,
one who surely deserves much greater things?

Respect and admiration, tenderness he gets.
Passion, lust, fulfilment. Contentment I believe.
I hope to make him happy
for this is what he needs.

I know these things I give him,
and pleasure this gives me,
so much, I want to love him,
if only I was free.

There lays a little corner deep within my heart,
where the love I still feel for you
is burning on and on.
So, release me from this feeling,
and let this love be gone.

To Die For You

I gave you both life,
the best investment I made.
No price could compare,
no miracle so divine,
the pleasures I get
from these offspring of mine.

I want you to know this. My message is clear.
I send it to you, who I hold most dear.
A good life I've had, I'm not greedy for I
know one day that I must surely die.

If my time is due
and you need my help.
If the grim reaper calls you,
I will say, "No, take me instead."
For I promise you both
I would not hesitate,
I will cry "Not them, take me,"
"To that pearly gate".

Sun, Moon, and Stars

Let's look up to the sun, moon, and stars.
Life is to be enjoyed!
Looking down on earth's clay and mud
does no more than sadden and depress.
Why waste this precious gift of life?
Look instead for happiness.

Life is not a dress rehearsal,
a time to practice for reincarnation.
Looking into crystal balls
will not solve problems or take away pain.
So, grab this life, squeeze it tight,
to waste this gift is such a shame.

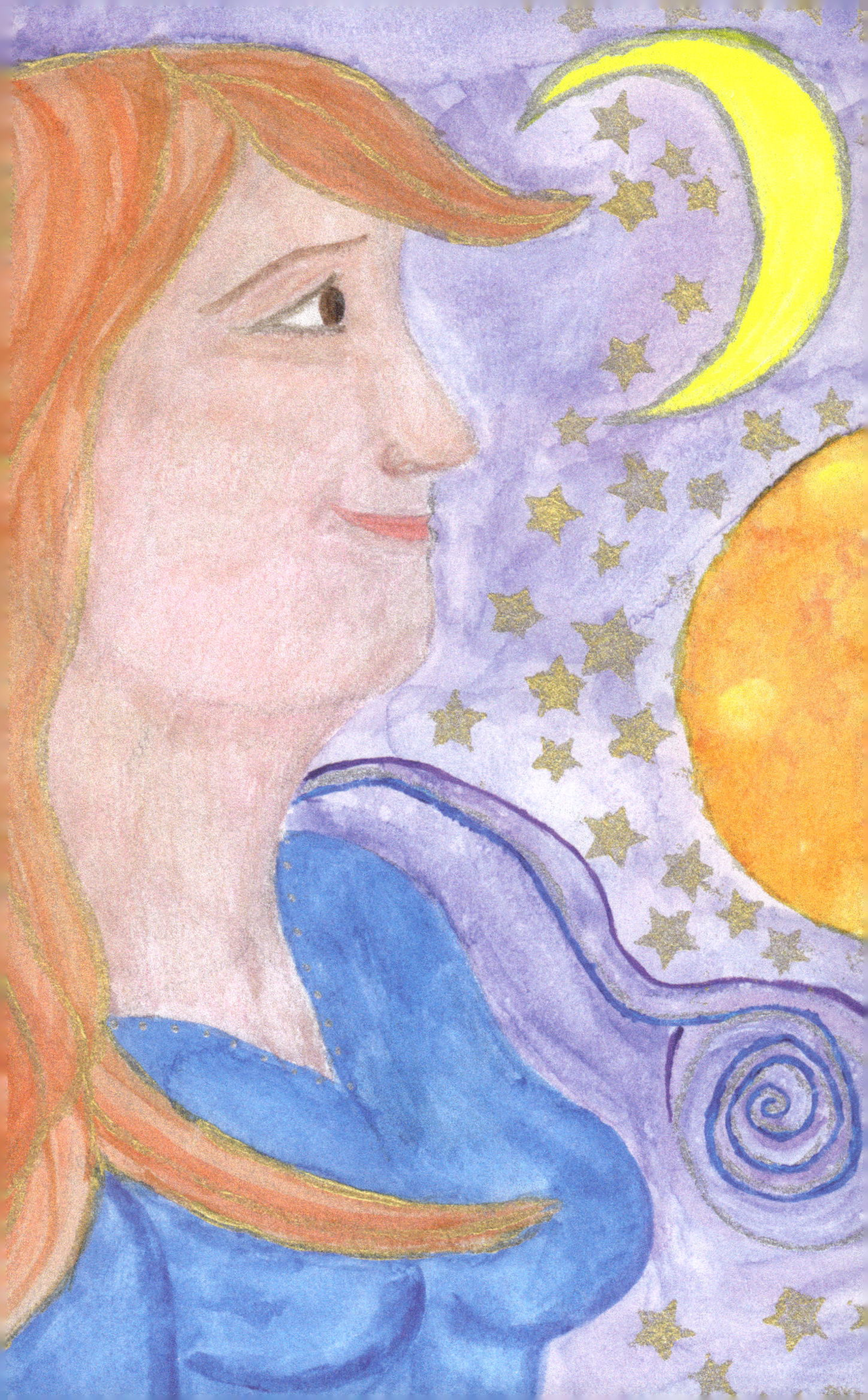

Confusion

Thoughts, feelings, meanings, turning in my head.
Analogous with clothes, in the machine going round.
Decisions, debates, conclusions to be drawn.
Brain cells stretched, bursting membranes fragile.
Swirling, sickening, dizziness and lights.
Springs tight in my head, causing sleepless nights.

Choices to make, feelings to spare.
Love to give you, if only I dare!
Spoilt for choice, who would have thought?
Responsibilities for others. Advice it is sought.

Still on the treadmill, but not in a cage.
Escape from reality, daydream, and smile.
Have patience, serve time, relax be calm.
Let destiny happen.
Do others no harm.

Magnetism

Feel the power, feel the pull,
drawn towards another being,
like gravity, pulling us down.
Negative pole are you -
positive am I.
Controlling the sea,
like a moon in the sky.

The centre of my earth, my heart,
is a magnet full of energy.
Powerful and strong.
To draw the negative pole to me
requires patience and skill,
earthly powers and destiny,
oceans of will.

Infection

A single cell,
Prokaryote, Bacteriophage,
Virus, that's what you are!
Invading my body, my mind, my soul.
Multiplying at a constant rate - no lag.
Occasionally, I allow myself into remission,
this is when the contact stops.
When your voice, I don't hear, or the mention of your
name, these are the worst times of this infectious game.

Pathogenic organisms can maim and destroy,
creating a war within oneself.
The B cells and the T cells
cascade together against the infectious M.
This infection is not associated with glamour or success,
not even with a hint of joy or happiness.
No. this is pure chemistry of soul, invading every organ,
every tissue, every cell, circulating in the blood,
pooling in a well.

Deep in this well, the bottom far out of reach.
Antibiotics, immunisations, vaccines, no cure.
I will try them all!
Write me a prescription,
one to be taken three times per day.
I suspect, therapy will be prolonged,
many years in my case.
Mostly due to the stubborn nature of my heart,
for once this infection had started,
the memory will continue,
until death do us part?

Which One

Love me? Love me not?
Like the ebb and flow of the tide,
deep or shallow,
fast or slow.
These are answers you want to know.

Do I trust you?
I think not.
Deep or shallow,
fast or slow.
Ask the other if you want to know.

Did you ask her?
I think so.
Deep or shallow,
fast or slow.
Did she answer – yes or no?

Love her? Love her not!
You will break her heart.
Deep or shallow,
fast or slow.
Do I love you?

I know so.

Another Chapter Closes

My life is like a book,
a novel to be precise.
Until the end I know not whether it be
a happy ending or a tragedy.

In three short years my life has changed,
commencing with the night
reborn an individual,
instead of someone's wife.
Melancholy I sit,
pondering for a time,
no introduction needed,
I know just where to start,
this chapter begins with another broken heart.

Where do I go from here?
Not trusting any man,
conditioned into believing they are all the same.

This time it will take me longer
to join the mating game.

Catherine?'
free,' she answered,
with a bitterness she couldn't
to struggle against death, alone,
feel like death!'
came boldly in
its, by saying—
his son is dying
tell him!
is your substa
millions of st
describe Adonis
have left me
and see only death!
ange shadow.
every one, one
can every shadow lend.
and the counterfeit
d after you;
of beauty set,

Mind Reading

If I could read your mind,
climb inside your soul,
feel what you feel,
know what you know.

Then perhaps I could fulfil your dreams.
Think of me as your wishing well.
Look into my eyes as you would look into the water.

Say the words you wish to express,
whisper the secrets of your heart,
shout the frustrations of your emotions,
share your hopes and dreams.

And maybe,
just maybe,
I can bring you happiness.

Frustration

What do I want?
What are my desires?

The past was all so certain,
almost like following a path
with posts along the way,
each one a defined goal.

Then the goal posts in my life were moved,
or so it seemed.

In reality, all I took was a different route,
reading the maps or the moon and stars.
These did not light the path that led to you,
timing was the key - to our destiny.

Philosophy

Philosophical thoughts weave lightly through my head.
Socrates, Plato, Aristotle, Loveley - now that's a gem!
How dare one associate with such eminent men.
All great thinkers with deep intellectual minds,
delving into issues - others would not raise.
Thinking beyond reason,
reasoning beyond belief,
believing in the unbelievable.
Never searching for recognition or praise.

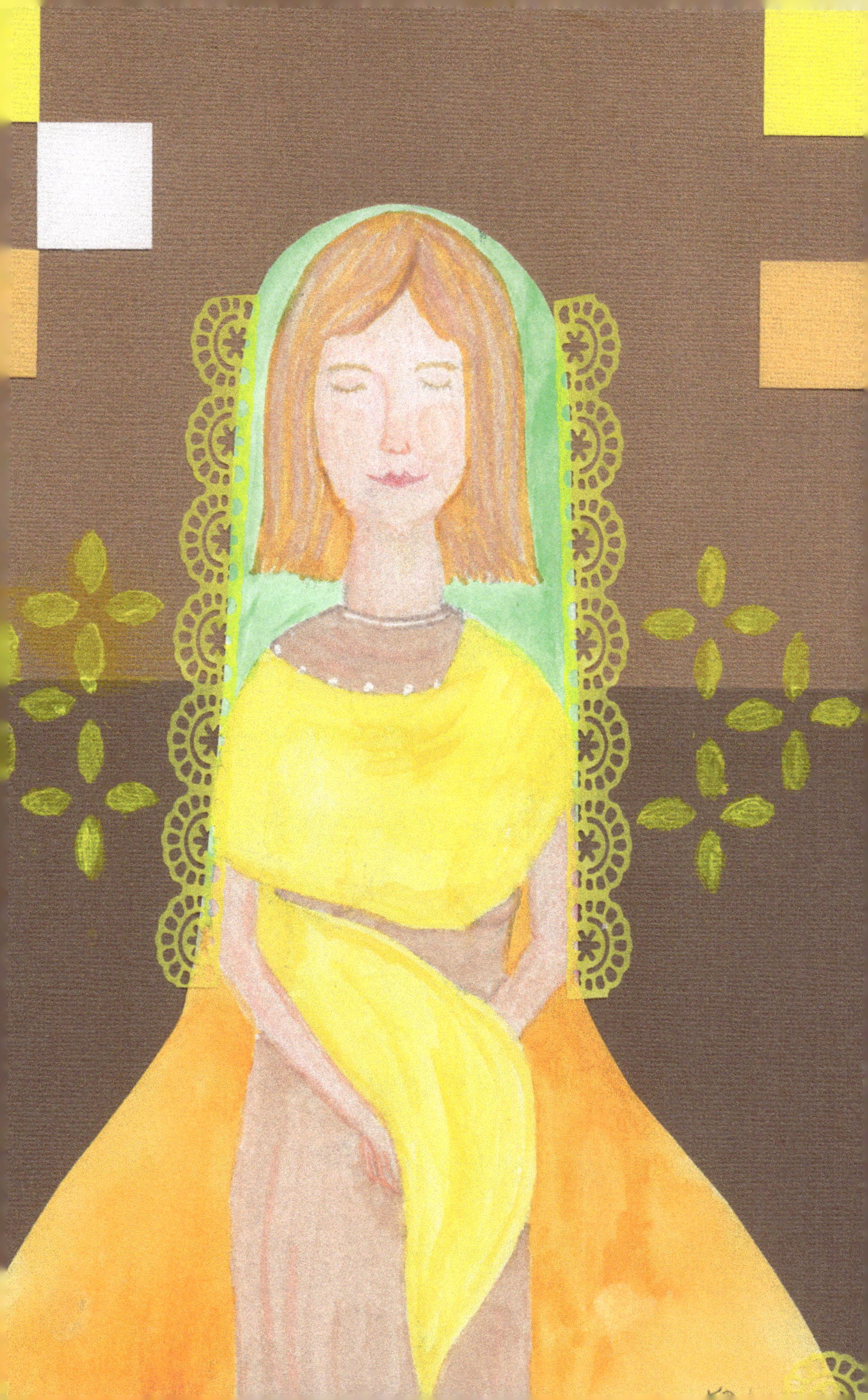

Children

Where are my children?
Where have they gone?
My house is just a house,
no longer a home.

Where is the music?
Where is the noise?
No shoes in the hall,
no coats on the pegs.

Washing basket empty,
no pots in the sink,
the cooker is clean, the fridge is empty.
Without my children, the house is empty and dull.

The beds are empty,
the cupboards are bear,
bathroom always available,
never anyone there.

Bereavement

Days like this should never happen.
Days like this should not occur.
Contented lives shattered.
Anguish, pain, despair.

Nine days since the celebration.
Dads seventy third year.
Always working, always busy.
Forever bringing in good cheer.

Was it sudden, or did he know?
Weeks of tiredness creeping on.
Feeling grumpy, feeling sad.
More than usual for my dad.

Sudden pain, mobility poor.
Struggling to move towards the door.
Let them in, he shouts to mum.
It may be daughters, it may be son.

His life surrounds the family.
With mum, his greatest love.
And now she loves him most of all.
She will forever be his turtle dove.

Vulnerable

Vulnerable - that's me.
Soft and sensitive to others feelings,
wanting to save the world,
persuaded by other's needs.

There you were.
I thought you were alone.
Big mistake, but all too late.
I was in love.
Attracted to your pheromones, charisma and wit.
You the candle, I the moth.

I tried to focus on other than the flame.
knew the dangers, hoped I wouldn't be burnt.
But the sabotage crept in,
the simmering intense,
the burn, the burn.

Are you man enough to extinguish the flames?
The flames your offspring have created.
Are you man enough to save your Queen?
I think you are.

Those Bones, Old Bones

"Calcium deposits," murmurs the young doctor,
with a sympathetic glance.
I nod my head,
subdued in an analgesic trance.
A careful hand draws near,
a calming voice to allay the fear.
Deep within my shoulder joint,
a stinging, sharp and piercing point.
Memories of pain, visualised and represented.
Sensations of tendons and ligaments cemented.
As water from the Trevi flows,
so, do my tears, my emotion grows.
Swaddled and strapped, sweating and grey,
I'm nearly a fossil, at the end of the day.

Decision Time

Your hands they move with that familiar gesture,
over and over you turn them,
looking for an imaginary wound,
but the wound is in your heart.

Inspection of your nails - just another guise,
this time to stare at your band of gold,
and hide the tears in your sad brown eyes.

Your silence hurts - I feel your pain,
I offer my hand again and again.
My own pain once acute is now chronic.
This moment has passed and travelled,
through my mind on a long journey to reach this day.

My brain has ached
thinking of ways to resolve this problem.
To you, I gave the lead.
I looked for answers, but you gave none.
Into the sand, you buried your head
like a child covering their head and expecting
invisibility.

Hopeful for resolution, without too much pain,
covering the same subject, again, and again.
The sands of time, through the hour glass flows,
forced into a decision.
Who stays? Who goes?

Moving On

Remember what I said,
as I felt the surge of frustration like a swollen river
run through my head.

Remember what I said,
as we lay together in our marital bed.

I wonder now! Did you take me serious?
Did you close your mind to avoid the pain?
Hoping the issue would melt away,
like snow when attacked by rain.

Remember what I said,
I wouldn't make you choose,
I would make it easy, smooth away the pain.
Iron away the creases,
then we can start again.

Olfactory Delights

Birth, babies, beautiful smell.
Sweet and warm, milk and honey.
Creamy texture, delicate skin.
Fragrance lovely, when life does begin.

The milky vomit, though sour is cute.
The Johnsons bath in a birthday suit.
The nappy, wet and heavy hung.
Still fragrant, no nostrils stung.

Children young, run wild and free.
Sticky hands and dirty face.
School room smells, polish, and soap.
Sponge and nail brush, mums last hope.

Teenage years, now that's a treat.
Smelly armpits, sweaty feet.
Spots on face, greasy hair.
Best not to mention unless it's a dare.

Fragrant years are now the start.
Perfume, aftershave to capture someone's heart.
Stale tobacco, peppermint smell.
Alcohol breath, tooth decay hell.

And finally, yes finally the smell to beat them all.
Ageing flesh, ageing bones.
Kidney failure, bladder weak.
Gastric gas, ulcers weep.
Flesh decayed. The final sleep.

Lazy Dave

He does as little as he can.
The effort needed to survive.
Is just enough to keep alive.

Bed and sofa make their call.
If not for money, he wouldn't work at all.
He does as little as he can.
Yet calls himself, a working man.

Observing others, he declares.
I am lucky, I have no cares.
I have a wife to cook for me.
Breakfast, lunch, and sometimes tea.

His washing done, his clothes are pressed.
The laundry fairy does her best.
The problem is, he needs to shave.
And sometimes shower, does lazy Dave.

But woe betide this lazy man.
Who does as little as he can.
One day he may find himself alone.
When his fairy flies, their grotto home.

Autumn Antics

Behind the secret garden
Behind the big stone wall.
Barry hears his calling.
Brian hears a fall.

Falling apples hit the ground.
Falling fruit, a thudding sound.
Falling down from laden bough.
Fruit for scrumping, here and now.

Come! Says Barry with a grin.
Come with me. Let's go in.
Can we climb a wall so high?
Calls Brian, with a heavy sigh.

And so they climb a wall so high.
Two young boys, brave and bold.
Like hero soldiers going forth.
To battle ground in times of old.

The smell of ripening fruit draws near.
They spy the apples on the ground.
In the distance.
Rosy red, big and round.

They leave the damaged apples.
And stuff their pockets tight.
With healthy shiny apples.
What fun, and such delight.

Shush! Says Brian. I hear a sound.
Of footsteps drawing near.
And sure enough, both boys found.
They were frozen still by fear.

Hello! Hello, the Policeman said.
Now what do we have here.
Are you Barry our Michaels lad?
Speak up and make it clear.

Yes Sir. I am. Barry replied.
A tremble in his voice.
The orchard is such a tempting place.
With fruit so tempting too.

And Sir! The fruit that we have picked.
Is for mam to make a pie for you.

Chameleon Days

Be seen, not heard, is what Mother said,
her wisdom spoken, from ancestors long dead.
Young ladies of breeding are quiet and reserved.
Always seen but never heard.

Show off your charms, use pastels and paints.
Kohl, pencils ink, perfume, cologne.
Wear what you think,
to capture the heart and mind of a beau,
always look pretty wherever you go.

Mothers words onto deaf ears fell.
Be seen and not heard, to me is obscene.
Why would I want to show off my charms?
Paint my face pretty, spray on the scent.

If I am not seen, if I am not heard.
I can quietly hide, listen, observe.
Look around, take my time.
Learn about life and the secrets it holds.

Go places, seek pleasure, wine, dine and dance.
Defer gratification for a fine romance.
Blend into the crowd, not noticed, not seen.
Camouflage complete, a chameleon's dream.

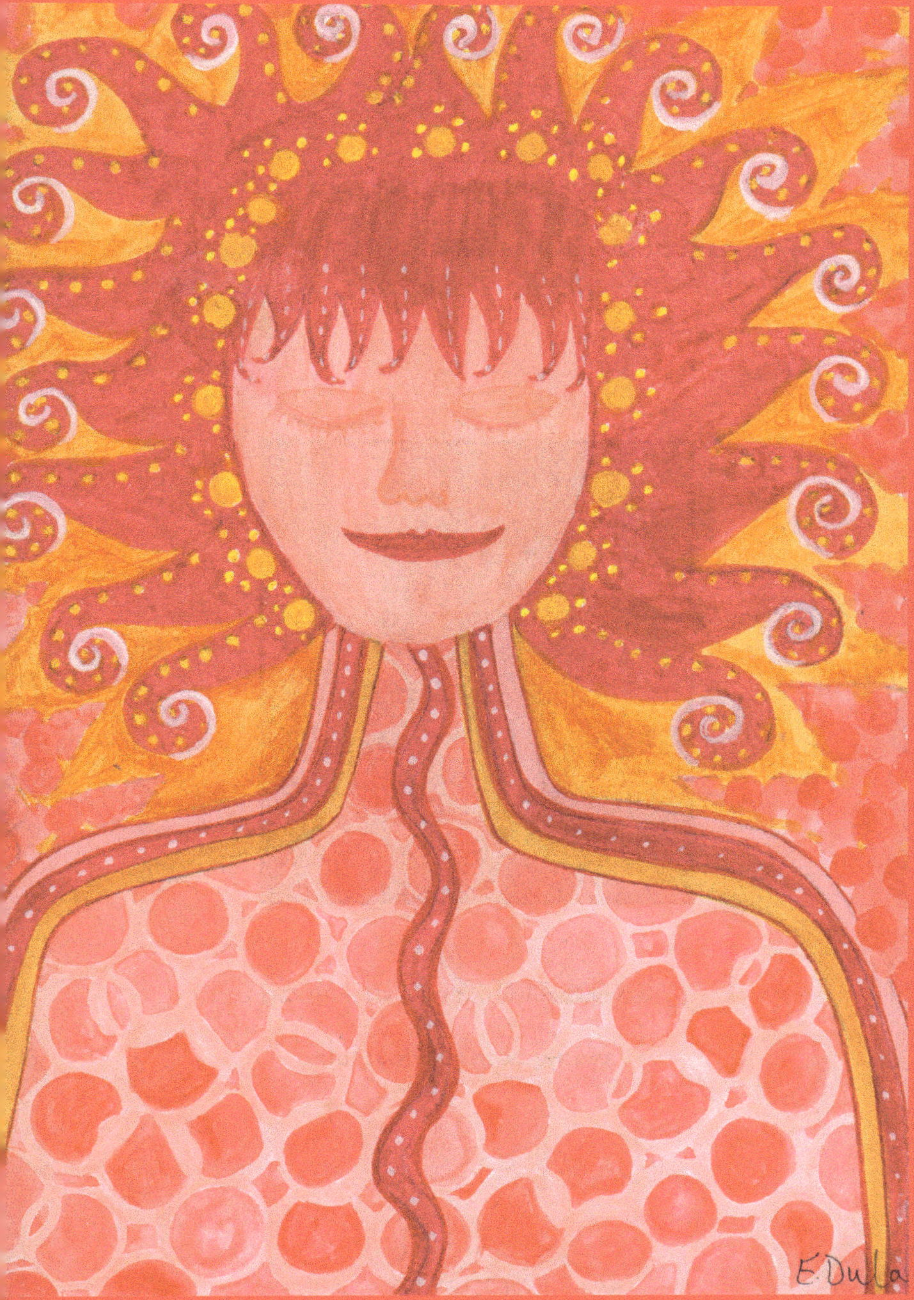
E.Dula

Elvina Dulac

Chameleon Days is beautifully illustrated by the Nottinghamshire artist Elvina Dulac. She is passionate about literature, theatre, and art. Elvina is a mixed-media artist and photographer who takes inspiration from the natural world.

www.facebook.com/sheistheart

twitter.com/ElvinaDulac

K.L. Loveley

K L. Loveley was born in Nottinghamshire in 1953. She began writing this collection of Poetry in 1997, a period of her life when she felt full of emotions and extremely philosophical about life.

She is the author of two novels, Alice published in February 2017 and Love, Secrets, and Absolution published in November 2017.

www.facebook.com/klloveley

twitter.com/K_L_Loveley

The Globeflower Agency

The Globeflower Agency provides a range of publishing and marketing services for authors, artists, and artisans.

www.globeflower.co.uk

www.facebook.com/theglobefloweragency

twitter.com/_Globeflower_

Lightning Source UK Ltd.
Milton Keynes UK
UKHW021139230119
336064UK00008B/121/P